Words of Wisdom 2

Compiled by Mark Ziaian

Published, 2020, by Transmedia Translating and Publishing Co., a branch of Intermedia Educational Co. Ltd, 2701-2 Forest Laneway, Toronto, Ontario, M2N 5X7. Phone: 1 647 454 0220. Email: intermediaeducational@gmail.com

Printed and distributed by Kindle Direct Publishing, Amazon

Ziaian, Mark (compiled by)
Words of Wisdom, Volume 2, 102 p + Index
Copyright 2020 Internationalmark
ISBN 978-1-896574-04-2

1. Quotes. 2. Proverbs. 3. Sayings. 1. Title

Cover: Mark Ziaian

I would like to thank everyone who sent in quotes to my interactive pages at www.internationalmark.co.uk

After almost two decades, I decided to take the quotes down and make them available in paperback.

All the quotes in this book are from my website sent in by members of the public and are by famous, infamous or even unknown people who wanted to share something with the world. Most of the sayings by unknown people cannot be found in any other publication.

I have tried to make as few changes as possible and publish what was originally sent to me. For this reason, some of the quotes will remain uncredited. Thus, the book is called "Words of Wisdom" and not "The Book of Quotes".

For practicality, *Words of Wisdom* will be published in two volumes. This is Volume 2.

Mark Ziaian

Words of Wisdom 2

"Gravity cannot be held responsible for people falling in love." - Albert Einstein

*****

"Always smile. Even just to a stranger, it may be the only sunshine they have seen all day."

*****

"His conscience was clear; he never used it."
- Stanislaw Jerzy Lec

*****

"That which does not kill us makes us stronger."
- Friedrich Nietzsche

*****

"For every minute that you are angry, you lose 60 seconds of happiness." - Ralph Waldo Emerson

*****

"If you love, give. If you see hurt cry, but if you see tears offer your time, because there is a place to pick for us all to reach out and wipe the tears of a hurting person. Did you miss your chance today?"
- Albert Camus

*****

"Love is life. And if you miss love, you miss life."
- Leo Buscaglia

*****

"Courage is not the lack of fear. It is acting in spite of it." - Mark Twain

*****

"Our greatest glory is not in never falling, but in rising each time we fall." - Confucius

*****

"You have to stand up for what you believe in, and sometimes that may mean standing alone."
- Tony Braxton

*****

"The way I see it, the more people that hate me, the less people I have to try to please." - Noel Gallagher

*****

"Pain is temporary, bragging right is forever."

*****

"Every perspective is different, but in the end, what we see is the same."

*****

"The part in giving up is not trying."

*****

"Love isn't who you dream of, it's who keeps you up thinking about them late at night. Because reality is better than any dream ever was"
*****

"Don't cry because it's over, smile because it happened." - Dr Seuss

*****

"The more you live, the less you die." – Janis Joplin

*****

"Life's a bi*** and then you die, so ***k the world and let's get high."

*****

"Someone somewhere Dreams of your smile, and in your presence they realize life is worthwhile. So when you are lonely remember it's true that somebody somewhere is thinking of you."

*****

"Whenever I fall in love, I fall for someone new but I always seem to find myself falling back in love with you."

*****

"My one regret in life is that I am not someone else." - Woody Allen

*****

"If you look back and replay your year and it doesn't bring you tears of joy or sadness than consider the year wasted."

*****

"Life is a journey, enjoy the ride."

*****

"Live life like no one is watching, it's funner that way." - Kathy Seida

*****

"Challenges build character."

*****

"There is no normal life, just life. So go out and get it!"

*****

"Sex is not the question. The question is do you want a ***k? The answer is Hell Yess."

*****

"True Love is spelled with 8 letters. Well, so is Bull S**t."

*****

"It is at the threshold of pain and suffering where the women are separated from the girls."

*****

"Life shrinks and Expands in proportion to one's courage." - Anaïs Nin

*****

"A male gynaecologist is like and auto mechanic who never owned a car." - Carrie Shaw

*****

"Do you know what's great about today? Nothing, wait for tomorrow."

*****

"Losers always whine about their best, winners go home an ***k the prom queen." - The Rock

*****

"Laughter is the best medicine." - The Bible

*****

"When you find out that the girl you like is taken, life sucks."

*****

"Winning isn't everything, it's the only thing."
- Vince Lombardi

*****

"It's all Greek to me." - William Shakespeare

*****

"Love with every second, care with every word, appreciate each day you have, give till it burns."
- Robert Dinges

*****

"When your luck is down and everything seems to be going wrong, just scream: sucklovey!"

*****

"If you hold on to the past, you will never get a grip on the future."

*****

"Know thy enemy" - William Shakespeare

*****

"Maybe our favorite quotations say more about us than about the stories and people we're quoting."
- John Green

*****

"I refuse to answer that question on the grounds that I don't know the answer" - Douglas Adams

*****

"Only fools fight in a burning house."
- Klingon proverb

*****

"Discovering yourself is a process in which God places tests before your morals, values, and overall relationship with him. Then having done that, you realize the type of person you are. Peace, blessings and most of all the love of God given to you all."

*****

"The world wants to be deceived." - Caleb Carr

*****

"The weak must fall to give rise to the strong"
- General Chang Klingon Academy

*****

"Better to be **ssed off than **ssed on."

*****

"What are friends? friends are just your enemies with secret identities."

*****

"At times we fear what the future holds, when in fact we carry the very cargo of the future on our backs today."

*****

"Fighting is a weak man's impulse."

*****

"The only man worth crying over is the one who will never make you cry."

*****

"Thou shall not shed new tears over old griefs."

*****

"The only person you must worry about is yourself."

*****

"Chicks before *icks."

*****

"Beauty is only skin deep."

*****

"There is no -i in team, but there is an -m and an -e."

*****

"Errors fly from mouth to mouth, pen to pen. To erase them takes ages." - Voltaire

*****

"Why spend all your money on material that will make you feel good for a couple of months, why not save the money and get plastic surgery and get a hot dude or gal that will last just as long as you"

*****

"Why live your life the way the media and all the pop culture tell you to? Just be yourself and you'll see how easy and fun life can really be."

*****

"If ur having a bad day. there's only one thing to do, tell yourself there's always other days."

*****

"The fish is wiser than the fish stick."

*****

"When two men in business always agree, one of them is unnecessary." - William Wrigley Jr

*****

"Go Trig Boy, It's Your Birthday!" - American Pie

*****

"Life is nothing more than what you make of it, for there is no turning back there is no backing out and there are no second chances. So don't forget this day because you will never be the same."

*****

"When life kicks you in the butt, turn around and kick it back."

*****

"Darkness cannot dive out darkness; only light can do that. Hate cannot drive out hate; only love can do that." - Martin Luther King JR.

*****

"Love is invisible until you see it in human form."

*****

"We live in an abnormal world and all kinds of things do exist, but this doesn't make them right."

*****

"Pain from loss is the deepest most incurable wound."

*****

"I'm not deprived, I just don't have a lot of stuff"
- Tommy D Katt

*****

"If all of my friends were to jump off a bridge, I wouldn't jump, I'd be at the bottom to catch them."

*****

"When the woman is around the set is down." - Becca

*****

"Think before you speak, if you speak before you think you won't know what you said." - Becca

*****

"Making one person happy, often times involves pi***ng another person off."

*****

"Don't take life too seriously, no-one ever comes out alive anyway."

*****

"I don't round that many girls cuz they talk too much."
- City High

*****

"Live and learn!"

*****

"Never spend too much time on an easy *ss two-minute speech."

*****

"You can fool some of the people all of the time, you can fool all of the people some of the time, you can never fool all of the people all of the time."
- Abraham Lincoln

*****

"Meddle not in the affairs of dragons, for you are crispy and taste like chicken."

*****

"I may not be there when you call me, but I'm going to be the first one to answer."

*****

"You can tell what a man fears most by what he uses to bring the fear out in you."

*****

"Highschool has been like a giant rollercoaster, it had its bumpy parts, but in the end, it was all worth the ride."

*****

"Mind over Matter; if you don't mind, it don't matter."

*****

"If Barbie is so popular, why do you have to buy her friends?"

*****

"If you wish to avoid looking at an idiot, break your mirror first." - François Rabelais

*****

"I know, it seems hard sometimes, but remember one thing, through every dark night, there's a brighter day after that. So, no matter how hard it gets, stick your chest out, keep your head up, and handle it."
- Tupac Shakur

*****

"Say what you mean, mean what you say, just don't say it mean."

*****

"I ain't a killer but don't push me, revenge is like the sweetest joy next to getting *ussy."- Tupac Shakur

*****

"Those who cannot obey cannot command."

*****

"If you hate love then you hate life and life isn't a thing to waste."

*****

"Freedom is only a state of mind."

*****

"Pain is temporary, pride is forever."

*****

"Never love anyone who treats you like you're ordinary." - Oscar Wilde

*****

"Imagination is the one weapon in the fight against reality."

*****

"Life is how you live it, so make the best of it, you only live it once"

*****

"Your inspiration is someone else's creation."

*****

"Whoever said it's better to have loved and lost, has never lost a love."

*****

"Don't you ever, in your mother ****ing life, when you know I got a gun, come at me with a knife."
- DMX

*****

"You may come to find that having is not so great a thing as wanting." - Spock

*****

"Life is like an onion; you discover it layer by layer and sometimes it makes you cry."

*****

"Very few things happen at the right time, and the rest do not happen at all: the conscientious historian will correct these defects." - Herodotus

*****

"Although I act as a clown, beneath this mask I'm wearing a frown." -The Beatles

*****

"Sarcasm is the root of all evil."

*****

"There is no point in hatred, there is too much time spent in hate. There is too much time spent killing. Work out your differences and love thy neighbor."

*****

"Go to bed with an itchy rear and wake up with a smelly finger."

*****

"You take freedom for granted until freedom is taken from you."

*****

"You live your life but once, love it in all its greatness and fight through its problems."

*****

"Love your enemies, they can easily turn into your friends."

*****

"Things are just there."

*****

"It is better to live one day as a lion than 100 days as a sheep."

*****

"Love is a game for two. The only real way you know it's real love, is if someone doesn't get hurt in the end."

*****

"Don't make fun of people. God could have easily made you just like them."

*****

"God didn't make people so we could hate them."

*****

"The best gift I ever got was forgivable sin and everlasting love. What's yours?"

*****

"If God doesn't hold grudges, I can do the same."

*****

"Beauty's where you find it, not just where you bump and grind it." - Madonna

*****

"Only boys that save their pennies, make my rainy day." - Madonna

*****

"Fashions can be bought, style one must possessed."

*****

"Play hard, have fun. Always cheat!"

*****

"Dreams come true; without that possibility, nature would not incite us to have them." - John Updike

*****

"Reach for the moon, if you fall short you will still be among the stars."

*****

"The hardest thing to do is to watch the person you love, love somebody else."

*****

"A man can kill one man on the street and be a murderer, but a man can kill 100 men in war and be a hero."

*****

"I never let school get in the way with my education."

*****

"Life's a bi***, and then you marry one."

*****

"Life is simply a fallacious appeal to the hypothetical."

*****

"I eat poo because poo taste good. If we all ate poo no-one would ever go hungry"

*****

"There are two things in the world that you don't go cheap on; airplane parts and birth control."

*****

"Remember Grant, remember Lee, the heck with them, Remember ME!"

*****

"Remember not everyone is going to love you."

*****

"If the #2 pencil is #1 in the nation, how come it is still #2?"

*****

"My boyfriend once told me to choose between him and shopping. I missed him at first."

*****

"If somebody doesn't like you, its Ok because in the future it won't matter because they won't be the one

you marry if they don't like you, they were not meant
for you."

*****

"If you use ruled paper, write with a broken pencil."

*****

"Never underestimate the power of Human stupidity."
- Robert A Heinlein

*****

"Have fun in the sun Get laid in the shade."

*****

"I can accept failure; everyone fails at something, but
I can't accept not trying."

*****

"Between two evils, I always pick the one I never tried
before." - Gwen Stefani

*****

"Live today like it is the end of the world."
- Leslie Bibb

*****

"No act of kindness, no mater how small, is ever
wasted." - Mother Teresa

*****

"All animals except man knows the ultimate of life is to enjoy it." - Samuel Butler

*****

"Try, try and try and if u can't do it give up!"

*****

"I hit big or miss big. I like to live as big as I can."
- Babe Ruth

*****

"The heart is not judged by how much you love but by how much you are loved by others." - Wizard of Oz

*****

"Whatever doesn't kill you can only make you stronger. No pain no gain."

*****

"An Army of sheep led by a lion will overcome an army of lions led by sheep." - Arab proverb

*****

"Jesus loves you, but the rest of the world doesn't, so watch out!"

*****

"Fill what's empty, empty what's full, and scratch where it Itches."

*****

"Mistakes are only mistakes if you don't learn from them, but when you learn from a mistake it becomes a lesson."

*****

"I never made a mistake in my life only learned lots of lessons."

*****

"They say love is blind, but I can't see to tell you. If you find it, let me know. Because I only want to know the difference."

*****

"Change is a good thing, but sometimes good things go bad."

*****

"Life is like a winding road always changing never staying in one spot."

*****

"I'm not afraid of computers taking over the world they're just sitting there, I can hit them with a two by four."

*****

"Perfection is achieved by those who aren't."

*****

"Believe you can do anything you want to do if you really put your heart, soul and mind into it."

*****

"You're born, then there's life, then you die. If you waste life, you've been dead since birth."

*****

"The next time Satan reminds you of your past remind him of his future."

*****

"Some mutha ***kas are always trying to ice-skate uphill." - Wesley Snipes, Blade

*****

"If I dream, you say I'm soft. If I don't, you say I'm heartless. So instead of showing my face, I just hide behind a person who doesn't cry."

*****

"One day you will ask me what is more important me or your life. You will walk away not knowing you are my life."

*****

"You thought I would play your game. You thought, but thinking isn't good enough."

*****

"To win you have to know. You know, you just choose to ignore the truth."

*****

"God bless the unblessed and kiss the hearts of the rest. Love Y'all," - Cheryl

*****

"The honor in a day comes from your heart not your purse."

*****

"In the fight between you and the world, back the world." - Frank Zappa

*****

"If A is success in life, then A equals X plus Y plus Z. Work is X; Y is play; and Z is keeping your mouth shut." - Albert Einstein

*****

"If you ain't getting older, you're dead."

*****

"Smile now cry later!"

*****

"Save the Plankton, kill the whales!"

*****

"we have nothing to fear but fear itself."
- Franklin D. Roosevelt

*****

"Love, honour and money are needed to live, but only one can never be taken away."

*****

"Never say, "it's better to have loved and lost than never to have loved at all" until you've tried it. It's a hell of a lot harder to accept once you've lost someone that was your whole world."

*****

"Heaven doesn't want me and hell's afraid I'll take over."

*****

"Don't drink and drive, get high and fly!"

*****

"It's the friends that you can call at 4 a.m. that matter."
- Marlene Dietrich

*****

"The love of my life is the love between friends."

*****

"Friends are the bacon bits in the salad bowl of life."

*****

"Life happens. Either deal with it and move on, or tell someone who cares."

*****

"Don't knock something before you know anything about it. Satan is not worse than God he speaks for what you want not for putting yourself through misery for forgiveness."

*****

"If at first you don't succeed, then skydiving is not for you."

*****

"Death is the only guarantee we have in life."

*****

"It doesn't matter where you are coming from. All that matters, is where you are going." - Brian Tracy

*****

"Your goals are the road maps that guide you and show you what is possible for your life." - Les Brown

*****

"Review your goals twice every day in order to be focused on achieving them". - Les Brown

*****

"Without goals, and plans to reach them, you are like a ship that has set sail with no destination."
- Fitzhugh Dodson

*****

"You could say that even in darkness there is light, but when you're hurt or angry, you only see what you want to see."

*****

"Aim for the top. There is plenty of room there. There are so few at the top it is almost lonely there."
- Samuel Insull

*****

"To say that you will "try" means that you are allowed to fail."

*****

"Death is such a small price to pay to end the misery which is life."

*****

"Anger brings hurt, hurt brings fear, fear destroys you."

*****

"I keep hearing that our destiny we create. That would be so wonderful if it were true cause if it were then I would for sure be loved by you. I want a man with depths like mine and there you are. looking too and I am not too far. I Will Love you forever if it exists but if you wound my soul forever is how long you'll find love a wish. Words from a witch when written are set in stone."

*****

"True happiness comes from forgiveness. If you can't learn to forgive and forget you can't live a truly happy life."

*****

"Sitting on our backside isn't going to get you very far in life; instead live your dreams because to dream a dream of life is only ever a dream to act a dream in life, life becomes."

*****

"Never lie to yourself; lie to others. But lie to yourself and forget who you are."

*****

"God says revenge is wrong, Satan says why the hell not revenge is such a sweet thing."

*****

"Death does not bring the end it brings back a memory long forgotten and so renews the life of a loved one into your heart and soul."

*****

"Death brings a renewal for the soul, takes it away from the old body and puts it in a newer one."

*****

"We all breath the same air, so learn to share!"

*****

"Love exists only as the mind says it does. Love is dead."

*****

"He who says magic does not exist has lost his soul and faith that he exists. 'If you cannot see it, it is not there' is that true? If so, how does a blind man know anything exists? He feels it. Magic can be felt if you try."

*****

"Fear; you can either let it destroy you or destroy your fear and become the stronger for it."

*****

"Even though you quit quitting you're still a quitter because while quitting quitting you quit."

*****

"A peach is a peach a plum is a plum but a kiss isn't a kiss without some tongue so open your mouth and close your eyes and give you tongue some exercise."

*****

"Oh what a beautiful morning, oh what a beautiful day. I've got a beautiful feeling, everything's going my way." - Oklahoma the musical

*****

"Do your best today for tomorrow you want to look back and be proud of the person you were."
- Henry Cloud

*****

"A picture is worth a thousand words but a picture of someone you love is worth the world."

*****

"Live Today like it was your last day because some day the day you call today will be your last."

*****

"The giant killer gorillas are coming, so don't worry about it."

*****

"Television is an invention that permits you to be entertained in your living room by people you wouldn't have in your house. - David Frost

*****

"Fight the good fight, live the good life, but in the end whether you like it or not you die the good death."

*****

"Cocaine and weed can still be legal all you have to do is convince more than half of USA's Population to back you up."

*****

"If you are reading this you're going to die. Face it."

*****

"Education is an admirable thing, but it is well to remember from time to time that nothing that is worth knowing can be taught." - Oscar Wilde

*****

"Women need to be beautiful to be loved by men, and stupid enough to love them." - Coco Chanel

*****

"A friend in weed is a friend indeed."

*****

"God gave you life and someday you're going to give it back."

*****

"You're only as good as you allow yourself to be."

*****

"1 tequila 2 tequila 3 tequila FLOOR,

1 tequila 2 tequila 3 tequila Grab all the tequila bottles you can carry and run out of the bar without catching attention."

*****

"I call a man, one who is master of his tongue."
- Don Lorenzo Milani

*****

"He who wishes to perish simply gives up."

*****

"If at first you don't succeed try again with weed."

*****

"Judging only wastes time and time is precious."

*****

"Cowards die many deaths but the brave only die once." - Ernest Hemingway

*****

"What luck for rulers that men don't think."
- Adolf Hitler

*****

"The only way to a peace on earth is to unite and be one; fighting is the last resort of the brain dead."
- Jace

*****

"It is easier to focus on the one brown patch, rather than the extent of green lawn around it."

*****

"May you live as long as you want, but not want as long as you live."

*****

"The line is only as fast as the very first person."

*****

"I don't try to do anything, either I do it or I don't."

*****

"History is the unfolding of miscalculation."

*****

"Smile! It makes people wonder what you're thinking."

*****

"No God, no peace, know God, know peace."

*****

"Life is a lost war; you can only try to win a few battles to forget those you have lost. A lost battle is only truly lost if the will to fight is broken and the knowledge is gone. Ultimately we are all losers."

*****

"Knowledge is power but ignorance is bliss, which would you rather have?"

*****

"Some say the mind bends and twist in order to deal with the horrors of life, sometimes the mind bends so much it snaps in two." - Twisted Metal: Black

*****

"Don't look backwards while you're walking forward or you will miss what's in front of you."

*****

"If God won't make me skinny please make all my friends fat."

*****

"The fool thinks himself to be wise, but the wise man knows himself to be a fool." - William Shakespeare

*****

"Be yourself and not what others want you to be."

*****

"Don't worry about your life, cause if you hold it too close you may lose it." - Rebecca St. James

*****

"Never go back. We're not meant to go back, which is why tomorrow never ends and yesterday is always gone." - Meredith

*****

"Rejection, my friends, is the key to ultimate success."

*****

"Tough titty said the kitty but the milk's still good."

*****

"Eternal sadness may fill your heart, but your hearts clouds will one day part. Another day another love, believe in yourself and the lord above."

*****

"I'd rather be poor and happy, than sad and rich."
- Andrea

*****

"If you let the heavens cry for you, your cheeks will stay dry, but if you let your eyes cry for you, your heart will stand by."

*****

"A secret is only safe between two people if one of them is dead."

*****

"The only true friend you will ever have is your shadow."

*****

"If you sit by the river long enough the bodies of your enemies will float past" - Sun Tzu

*****

"If you meet this wonderful guy and you hear his name and you remember hearing a ton of girls say that name several times before don't think he's so wonderful anymore because you will soon find out he wasn't anyone you want to go for. Because once a cheater always a cheater."

*****

"Foolishness is bound up in the heart of a child, but the rod of correction will drive them far from it."
- The Holy Bible

*****

"They came for the Jews and I did not say anything for I was not a Jew. They came for the blacks and I did not say anything for I was not black. They came for the gays and I did not say anything for I was not gay. They came for me and there was no one left to say something for me."

*****

"Live life to its fullest, you're not getting out alive anyway."

*****

"S**t happens, then you die."

*****

"Never complain over things you are willing to tolerate."

*****

"In any moment of decision, the best thing you can do is the right thing. The worst thing you can do is nothing." - Theodore Roosevelt

*****

"My tears are like diamonds; no man is worth them."

*****

"It's hard to find yourself, when you're not sure who you're looking for."

*****

"The trouble with this country is that there are too many politicians who believe, with a conviction based on experience, that you can fool all of the people all of the time." - Franklin Pierce Adams

*****

"Do not regret my fate; if I have consented to survive, it is to serve your glory." - Napoleon

*****

"Friendship is a disinterested commerce between equals; love, an abject intercourse between tyrants and slaves." - Oliver Goldsmith

*****

"Imagination is more important than knowledge."
- Albert Einstein

*****

"We, and all others who believe in freedom as deeply as we do, would rather die on our feet than live on our knees." - Franklin D. Roosevelt

*****

"If a man hasn't found anything he will die for he isn't fit to live."

*****

"Risk more than others think is safe. Care more than others think is wise. Dream more than others think is practical. Expect more than others think is possible."
- Cadet Maxim

*****

"Time; alas, there is no way to recover lost time, but you learn to make use of what is left once you realize what you have lost."- Yvonne Hugli

*****

"What's right isn't always popular, and what's popular isn't always right."

*****

"I disapprove of what you say, but I will defend to death your right to say it." - Voltaire

*****

"It is history that teaches us to hope." - Robert E. Lee

*****

"As for life, it is a battle and a sojourning in a strange land; but the fame that comes after is oblivion."
- Marcus Aurelius "

*****

"The Christian resolution to find the world ugly and bad has made the world ugly and bad."
- Friedrich Nietzsche

*****

"When you have tried so very hard and the pain is too much to bear, don't worry it's just the weakness leaving your body."

*****

"They may forget what you said, but they will never forget how you made them feel." - Carl W. Buechner

*****

"Don't go around saying the world owes you a living. The world owes you nothing. It was here first."

- Mark Twain

*****

"The universe is change; our life is what our thoughts make it." - Marcus Aurelius

*****

"If love isn't a game, then why are there so many players?"

*****

"The hardest battle in life is to be yourself in a world that night and day, is trying to make you like everyone else."

*****

"No-one likes change except wet babies."
- Mark Twain

*****

"Only a life lived for others is worth living."
- Albert Einstein

*****

"Don't eat yellow snow!"

*****

"Next time I see you, remind me not to talk to you."

- Groucho Marx

*****

"Experience can be the hardest teacher, it gives you the test before the lesson." - Angelo Selva

*****

"At the end of the day, all the pieces go in the same box, kings and pawns alike." - Father Bernie Rossi

*****

"Live life to its fullest, not by everyone else's standards."

*****

"If you're going to talk about me than tell it to my face."

*****

"Don't be a poser; be yourself."

*****

"I want to learn."

*****

"People always complain about the rain, but they never complain about the flowers." - Ana Paredes

*****

"What is upper homie?"

*****

"If we lose money, we can always earn it back, if we lose a minute it is lost forever." - Ana Paredes

*****

"Hi, I'm Satan, enjoy the film." - Crow T. Robot

*****

"Naked fun is good fun."

*****

"Never trust anything that bleeds for five days without dying."

*****

"Give yourself over to absolute pleasure."
- Rocky Horror Picture Show

*****

"What is it about the gates of hell that causes people to want to wander into them?" - Crow T. Robot

*****

"If u think playing the game is hard, try riding the bench."

*****

"Don't live for the future, don't cry for the past, but live for the moment, the moment will not last."

*****

"It is not who you are today but who you will become tomorrow." - Chitown

*****

"Your sense of self is not based on someone else's perceptions of you but on how you value yourself."

*****

"I've soared to the heavens on the wings of eternity, and fallen to the shores of forgiveness, through this journey I've learned many things, the most pertinent being, thine eyes do deceive, and life is but a sickness." - Alex Perkins

*****

"To be or not to be? That is the question."
- William Shakespeare

*****

"As long as there's a life to live, there's always a heart to give."

*****

"Your past always comes back and kicks you in the **s."

*****

"The future belongs to those who believe in the power of their dreams." - Eleanor Roosevelt

*****

"Die and you will live, in a world that has much more to give."

*****

"Before there are successful adults, there are kids with potential."

*****

"When you are faced with a difficult decision, take the more challenging one because you will get a larger reward." - Gwen Murphy

*****

"The world is a beautiful place, live your life as you wish and hope that all your dreams will come true, because you can make them."

*****

"I do not feel obliged to believe that the same God who has endowed us with sense, reason, and intellect has intended us to forgo their use." - Galileo Galilei

*****

"Do, or do not. There is no try." - Yoda

*****

"My heart is like a puzzle; I give you a piece every day. When it is finished it is yours to keep."

*****

"No-one is worth your tears, and the one that is, won't make you cry."

*****

"I know there's other fish in the sea, but I lost my pole when the other one got away from me."

*****

"Live a long and happy life, just don't live mine."

*****

"Keep in mind that a moment only lasts so long and that once it's gone you can never get it back."

*****

"With age you get wrinkles, but luckily your eyesight gets worse so you can't see them." - Mark Ziaian

*****

"If you love something let it go, If it comes back to you it's yours, if it doesn't it never was."
- Tupac Shakur

*****

"One hand washes the other."

*****

"You can't change the past, but you can change the future."

*****

"When life gives you lemons, make lemonade."

*****

"When I turned around everything changed."

****

"Love is blind. I guess that's why no one has seen me."

*****

"I may be as bad as hell but when I'm with you I'm as good as you can tell."

*****

"How can you love others if you don't love yourself?"

*****

"A consensus means that everyone agrees to say collectively what no one believes individually."
- Abba Eban

*****

"A great doing is doing what others say you cannot achieve."

*****

"Don't teach a pig to sing, it not only wastes your time but also annoys the pig."

*****

"What you don't see with your eyes, don't invent with your mouth."

*****

"Love can sometimes be magic but remember magic can sometimes be an illusion."

*****

"Death is not the end, it's only just the beginning."

*****

"Nobody is perfect until you fall in love with them."

*****

"The worst feeling is to watch someone you love, love somebody else."

*****

"What do you do when the only person who can make you stop crying, is the one who made you cry?"

*****

"Any intelligent fool can make a thing bigger more complex and more violent, but it takes a lot of courage and a touch of genius to move in the opposite direction."

* * * * *

"Don't bother crying over anyone who won't cry over you."

* * * * *

"Best friends are hard to find, harder to leave and impossible to forget."

* * * * *

"I'm just going to get my feet wet until I drown."

* * * * *

"Things get worse before they get better."

* * * * *

"Instead of looking for the right road to travel on; make your own but make sure to leave a trail, for you may realize that the road you created for yourself was the perfect one for you, instead of the other road that was created for someone else."

* * * * *

"Fear leads to anger, anger leads to hate, hate leads to suffering." -Yoda

* * * * *

"Advice is what we ask for when we already know the answer but wish we didn't."

*****

"When dreaming of great things in life you have to remember to open your eyes to see what's in front of you."

*****

"You ain't cool unless you pee your pants."
- Adam Sandler

*****

"People put stuff off, thinking they will do it later. What if there is no later?"

*****

"Absolute power leads to absolute tyranny."

*****

"Live life to the fullest don't wait to the last minute to tell someone how you feel about them, cause you don't want it to be too late." - Lillian

*****

"life's short so don't die!" - Lillian

*****

"Man makes the decisions that make the man."

*****

"In love we often doubt what we most believe."

*****

"War has knocked some of the world's greatest men to their knees and lifted men from their knees to greatness."

*****

"Movies don't create psychos; they just make psychos more creative." - Scream

*****

"The smallest hint of self-interest corrupts the purest of leaders."

*****

"Someone once said that you must forget and live life to the fullest and to the future."

*****

"Death, the end of one story, only a chapter in everyone else's".

*****

"To crawl, one must first comprehend "want" and realize the necessity for an independent means of obtaining."

*****

"If you don't have time to do it right the first time

where are you going to find the time to do it right the second time?"

*****

"Being smart is knowing what you're dumb at."

*****

"If you pray for rain be prepared for mud."

*****

"Knowledge is only important if you know nothing."

*****

"It's easier to yell an insult than to throw a helping hand."

*****

"Live life like there was no yesterday and there is no tomorrow."

*****

"Freedom is chaos with better lighting."

*****

"Love sucks deal with it."

*****

"People make it easy to hate them."

*****

"Blessed are those who expect little, for they will never be disappointed."

*****

"If you have to step on people to get ahead, well they shouldn't have been there."

*****

"The Bible isn't everything; do what your mom told u to."

*****

"The advice that is wanted is commonly not welcome and that which is not wanted, evidently an effrontery."
- Samuel Johnson

*****

"Make love not war."

*****

"Respect yourself and your body, God gave you one body."

*****

"Love each other!"

*****

"No greater distance can separate two lovers, as the heart knows no concept of proximity."

*****

"Only when the color of our skin is like the color of our eyes will there be no more war."

*****

"Hippies smell." - A bumper sticker

*****

"A small mind is easily filled with faith."

*****

"There is no arguing with the barrel of a gun."
- Ancient proverb

*****

"I stare into my baby daughter's eyes with amazement attempting to solve her thoughts and wonders. She appears so full of life and love. And its then that I realize with a half-made grin. It's the outpouring of a proud father shining back at me."

*****

"You know enough to know nothing." - Socrates

*****

"A person with no goals makes no mistakes."

*****

"Guys are like stars; there are millions of them out there but only one will make your dream come true."

*****

"Having cannons in your army don't guaranty the victory, but if you stay in front of them you will certainly lose the battle."

*****

"You gotta hurt in order to know, fall in order to grow, lose in order to gain, cuz most of life's lessons are learned in pain." - Joan

*****

"Every new day is worse than the last so essentially tomorrow will be the worst day of my life."

*****

"I will let no man narrow or degrade me by making me hate him."

*****

"You can live to be a hundred if you give up all the things that make you want to live to be a hundred."
- Woody Allen

*****

"You can be to the left of anything you like, but not of good sense." -Enzo Biagi

*****

"Infinite is forever."

*****

"Religion is like fire; respect it and it will keep you warm, disrespect it, and it will burn you."

*****

"Smile today because tomorrow will be worse."

*****

"There is no such thing as a mistake, just a life experience."

*****

"The more you try, the harder it gets."

*****

"Fat people are harder to kidnap."

*****

"When life seems to become more than you can handle, it's because you're not supposed to handle it alone."

*****

"The one who loves you will give you another chance."

*****

"for your own good' is a persuasive argument that will eventually make a man agree to his own destruction."
- Janet Frame

*****

"Turn your sand into gold."

*****

"Live and let live!"

*****

"If you're not wasted the day is."

*****

"With love time is not an issue, it's love's best friend."

*****

"A man spent his lifetime in finding a short cut to spend it."

*****

"There is nothing better than this, I now know what true love truly is."

*****

"Change the world, don't let the world change you."

*****

"We choose the value of our own lives."

*****

"Where there is will, there's a way, or a hell of a lot of alcohol."

*****

"We do not become better or worse with age, we simply become more of ourselves." -Gertrude Stein

*****

"Discipline yourself so others don't have to."

*****

"The more you love someone the more it hurts, the more it hurts the more you love."

*****

"It's not the dead you should be scared of it's the living."

*****

"Life's a b**ch deal with it."

*****

"Force is followed by loss of strength. This is not the way of nature. That which goes against nature comes to an early end."

*****

"Look but don't touch. Touch but don't taste. Taste but don't swallow."

*****

"What's better: A lie that makes you smile, or the truth that makes you cry?"

*****

"Obesity kills! Step away from the Burger and fries!"

*****

"Life is like a puzzle; you put detail after detail and have a beautiful picture, your own picture. And enjoy it! If you lose one detail, certainly it is sad, but you can draw it yourself at least to fill that void, to feel happier. Only your own built picture can be meaningful and significant."

*****

"Government is not reason. It is not eloquence, it is force, and like fire. It is a dangerous servant and a fearful master." - George Washington

*****

"Friends are one of life's most prized possessions. Never give them up without a fight."

*****

"Democracy is a device that ensures that we shall be governed no better than we deserve."
- George Bernard Shaw

*****

"The same words uttered by different mouths take on different, even antithetic, meanings."
- Alessandro Morandotti

*****

"My tears flow freely with that of my pen."

*****

"As I told you once, I will not let you go because by leaving you would lose everything."

*****

"Walking away is not cowardness, conforming because fear of rejection comes along is the lowest form of cowardness."

*****

"Suicide is not necessarily an act of cowardice, fear of death at the cost of freedom is." - John Hebert

*****

"To not know is bad, to not wish to know is worse."
- African proverb

*****

"The hero is the teller of the tale"

*****

"A child who is to be reared successfully is not to be reared on a bed of down." - Akan proverb

*****

"Democracy is the right to choose your dictator."
- Mark Ziaian

*****

"Nobody in this world is stupid, but if you act like you are, then you will be treated like you are."

*****

"The more I learn the less I know." - Beatles

*****

"Love conquers all." - Moulin Rouge

*****

"Hold your fears in your left hand, your right hand will deal with it when you put them together."

*****

"History is a weapon."

*****

"If you can't bear no crosses, you can't wear no crown."

*****

"The cost of liberty is less than the price of repression." - W.E.B. Du Bois

*****

"The mind is the greatest weapon known to man."
- Krystal Sundstrom-Hebert

*****

"Do not go into a game hoping that you are going to win go into a game wondering how much you're going to win by."

*****

"The pen is mightier than the sword."

*****

"Believe none of what you hear and half of what you see." - Benjamin Franklin

*****

"Suicide is painless." - M*A*S*H

*****

"We are all here to learn lessons, and the world is our teacher."

*****

"We have just enough religion to make us hate, but not enough to make us love one another."
- Jonathan Swift

*****

"When you fight life, life always wins."

*****

"If it doesn't matter who wins and loses then why do they keep score?"

*****

"A girl who has her feet firmly planted on the ground cannot put her pants on."

*****

"It's only when you have lost everything that you are free to do anything."

*****

"Everything has a negative and positive side to it. If you only see the positive in everything, then you are blinding yourself to reality. Weigh out the positive and negative. If there is too much negative, then you need to get rid of it. Because, it is not working."

*****

"Everyone wakes up in the morning hoping to have a wonderful day. My philosophy behind it all is don't sweat the small stuff. You're only as happy as you want to be." - Jake Dickson

*****

"You are a liar Sir!"

*****

"With the distance of origin lies the betrayal of truth."

*****

"Not all who wander are lost."

*****

"The wind was warm the trees were bare and the moon illuminated the ground which was, our dance floor."

*****

"Slow down! The thing you're rushing to may not be as important as the thing you're passing by."

*****

"Love and time are the only two things in the world that can be spent but can't be bought."

*****

"A man with many fears is troubled, a man with none is a liar."

*****

"It's better to seize and engage your life than to die alone and unhappy."

*****

"Every man dies, but not every man lives."
- Braveheart

*****

"In the end, it just comes down to one thing. You can't run from the wind. You face the music. You trim your sail. And you keep going." - White Squally

*****

"All there is to thinking is seeing something noticeable which makes you see something you weren't noticing which makes you see something that isn't even visible." - Norman Maclean

*****

"Grow up, but don't do it too fast. You will only be young once in your life."

*****

"I cannot manage the pressures of patrons, let alone paint." - Michelangelo

*****

"Nearly all men can stand adversity but if you want to test a man's character, give him power."
- Abraham Lincoln

*****

"Welcome pain. Being able to feel sorrow and pain assures you that you can feel happiness and love."

*****

"Don't burn old bridges; you would be surprised how many times you will have to cross them again.

*****

"The University of Failure has taught me how to overcome the greatest and most insurmountable odds.

Thank God for the process of overcoming and learning through failure."

*****

"Do not possess your weaknesses, prevail and gain even more sanity."

*****

"There are a lot of males in this country called the U.S.A but very few men."

*****

"What is your worth if you can't look yourself in the eyes and see your own conviction."

*****

"A dreamer is never understood and will never be, because he marches to the beat of a different drum."

*****

"A man's heart is filled with passion when he is serving his fellow man."

*****

"Character is the hunger and desire to finish what one starts."

*****

"So few people give up on what they say they believe so strongly in. Maybe there is a lack of guts or motivation."

*****

"The greatest trick the devil ever played was convincing the world he didn't exist."
- The Usual Suspects

*****

"It takes five seconds to become a champ but it takes a life time to act like one."

*****

"A bank is a place where they lend you an umbrella in fair weather and ask for it back when it begins to rain." - Robert Frost

*****

"An Ambassador is an honest man, sent to lie abroad for the good of his country." - Sir Henry Wotton

*****

"Pimping ain't easy but it sure is fun."

*****

"There is no right and wrong, there's only fun and boring" - Hackers.

*****

"Your ignorance cramps my conversation."
- Anthony Hope

*****

"As a well spent day brings happy sleep, so life well used brings happy death." - Leonardo Da Vinci

*****

"Hope is like a tree; it starts small, then it grows and branches into different directions. No-one knows when it will be fully grown, but when it is, it's a very beautiful tree."

*****

"The most incomprehensible thing about the world is that it is comprehensible." - Albert Einstein

*****

"Pick battles big enough to matter, but small enough to win." - Johnathan Kozol

*****

"God gave burdens, also shoulders." - Yiddish proverb

*****

"In love's war, only wounded soldiers may serve."

*****

"You reap what you sow." - The Bible

*****

"If you have built castles in the air, your work need not to be lost; that is where they should be. Now put foundations under them." - Henry Thoreau

*****

"Forget about finding happiness; happiness is not worth of your search." - Rich Mullins

*****

"This is how we know what love is; while we were still sinners Christ died for us." - The Bible

*****

"Happiness is often lost in the search for it" - Melanie

*****

"Madness is the first step to genius."

*****

"Science only serves to verify the discoveries of instinct." - Jean Cocteau

*****

"Fall seven times, stand up eight." - Japanese proverb

*****

"The dog wags his tail, not for you, but for your bread." - Portuguese proverb

*****

"An optimist hasn't had much experience."

*****

"Between men and Women there is no friendship possible. There is enmity, passion, worship, love, but no friendship." - Oscar Wilde

*****

"Whenever you are asked if you can do a job tell 'em "Certainly I can!" Then get busy and find out how to do it." - Theodore Roosevelt

*****

"When you throw dirt, you lose ground."
-Texan proverb

*****

"Don't marry someone you can live, with, marry someone you can't live without." - Josh McDowell

*****

"Victory is reserved for those who are willing to pay the price."

*****

"God created us, but the devil changed us."

*****

"I'm not interested in the possibilities of defeat."

*****

"Nothing is more difficult, and therefore more precious, than to be able to decide on the perfect girl."

*****

"Kisses blown are kisses wasted
Kisses aren't kisses unless their tasted
Kisses spread germs and germs are hated
So kiss me baby I'm vaccinated."

*****

"If you can't say something nice, don't say nothing at all." - Thumper

*****

"If I was two-faced would I be wearing this one?"

*****

"Footsteps in time are not made by siting down."

*****

"Live for the game life, and never forget people who talk bad about you are the people who wished they were you."

*****

"The difference between love and friendship is how much you can hurt each other."

*****

"The difficult thing in the world is giving in a simple form."

*****

"Good things come to those who wait, but only the things left by those who hustle."

*****

"It is not love that hurts it is the losing of love that hurts."

*****

"In a parallel universe suddenly divested of illusion and light, man meets an alien, a stranger, his exile is without remedy as he is deprived of the memory of a lost home or promised land."

*****

"It takes 42 muscles to frown; it only takes 6 muscles to extend your arm and B**** slap the mother f***er."

*****

"Love is a prerequisite for wisdom."

*****

"He (she?) was mad and he didn't know it; but he knew he didn't know." - Shodja Ziaian

*****

"If you could love me half as much as I love you then the whole world would stop and awe at the magnificence of your love for me."

*****

"Sometimes you feel it is hard being that person you don't like; yet you feel it is easy being the person you are not, so don't be quiescence and don't display pretence."

*****

"Don't be afraid to give your best to what seemingly are small jobs. Every time you conquer one, it makes you that much stronger If you do."

*****

"If you fall, stand tall, and come back for more."
- Tupac Shakur

*****

"Live life for yourself, and not for others, otherwise you are not truly being yourself." - Bobbi

*****

"There is no I in TEAM but there is a ME."

*****

"Many men try to walk in their father's footsteps; instead, try to forge your own." - Erin

*****

"There are many clichés in life, try not to be one!"

*****

"If a man does not keep pace with his companions, perhaps it is because he steps to the beat of a different drummer. Let him step to the music he hears, however measured or far away."

*****

"When you have to cope with a lot of problems, you have two options; you're either going to sink or you're going to swim."

*****

"A b**ch is a b**ch, but a dog is a man's best friend."

*****

"It's harder to get from here to there
If you set your goals too high;
Then nothing ever works out right;
Too soon you no longer try."

*****

"If you judge people you have no time to love them."
- Mother Teresa

*****

"Look around and choose your own ground for long you live and high you fly and smiles you'll give and

tears you'll cry and all you touch and all you see is all
your life will ever be." - Roger Waters

*****

"Those who have tried hard in their life, are more
experienced than those who have not once in their life
ever tried."

*****

"I don't know with what weapons World War III will
be fought, but World War IV will be fought with
sticks and stones." - Albert Einstein

*****

"Sunshine fades, and shadows fall, but sweet
remembrance outlasts all."

*****

"If you can't beat them, join them!"

*****

"When the rain is blowing in your face
And the whole world is on your case
I could offer you a warm embrace
To make you feel my love.
When the evening shadows and the stars appear
And there is no one there to dry your tears
I could hold you for a million years
To make you feel my love." - Billy Joel

*****

"We are the unwilling, led by the unqualified, to do the impossible, for the ungrateful. For so long, with so little, we are now qualified, to do anything, with nothing."

*****

"It's lack of faith that makes people afraid of meeting challenges, and I believed in myself."
- Muhammad Ali

*****

"If at first you don't succeed, quit or change the rules."

*****

"I can forgive, but not forget."

*****

"Somewhere there's someone who dreams of your smile,
And finds in your presence that life is worthwhile,
So, when you are lonely, remember this is true:
Somebody, somewhere is thinking of you."

*****

"An enemy is a friend yet to be made."

*****

"Accept life as it comes, it cannot be changed."

*****

"Love is that condition in which the happiness of another person is essential to your own."
-Robert A. Heinlein

*****

"Imagination is more important than knowledge, because without imagination there would be no knowledge."

*****

"Do not do, if you would undo if caught."

*****

"Don't fish in a cow field; all you will catch is bull s**t." - James Bowen

*****

"The bigger the stalk the higher you'll climb."
- James Bowen

*****

"There's a time and place for everything; and that's college."

*****

"You are always more important than anyone else, never let a guy be more important than yourself or you will be eating out of their hand which is not good."

*****

"Life is too short to live for tomorrow, so live for today."

*****

"Take advantage of life's little offers."

*****

"You don't own your life, your life owns you."

*****

"Respect everyone, because one day you may need a job."

*****

"A mind is useless, if the heart is gutter."

*****

"Begin each day with the words "I can do it" and end each night with the words "I did it.""

*****

"Never Go to bed mad or angry, because you may never wake up."

*****

"You're born into this world and they say you're born with sin. Well at least they gave me something, I didn't have to steal or have to win."

*****

"The less I have the more I gain."

*****

"From the day you're born you begin to die, so live life the way you want."

*****

"Shoot for the moon cause if you miss, you'll still reach the stars."

*****

"A man does not age when his skin is wrinkled, but when his dreams and hopes wrinkle. - From Spanish

*****

"Gravitation cannot be blamed for people falling in love."

*****

"All you need is love. But a little chocolate now and then doesn't hurt." - Charles M. Schulz

*****

"Sometimes the questions are complicated and the answers are simple." - Dr Seuss

*****

"The only way to get what you want, is to ask the person that knows."

*****

"They say that true lovers hold hands, but true lovers know that the other's hand is always there."

*****

"Love those who love you."

*****

"There is no greater agony than bearing an untold story inside you." - Maya Angelou

*****

"The only foolproof way to know what you want is to see what you have."

*****

"Love is like a gamble. You either gain from it or lose it."

*****

"Trust no one other than yourself as "you" are the only person in this world who will never betray you."

*****

"If I was a man, I could swim that fast."
- Amy Van Dyken

*****

"Everything you can imagine is real." - Pablo Picasso

*****

"When I die and look back on my life, I will not regret the things that I did, but those that I did not do."

*****

"The people who call me strange are those who live their lives in fear."

*****

"If it hurts then don't do it."

*****

"Smoke weed not people."

*****

"Words are easier said than done."

*****

"This is your world; I just got me a room in it."

*****

"The world is full of miracles some big, some small, some that happen all at once and some take time to develop and it's those that take time to grow that are the most important to treasure and protect."

*****

"Experience is the best teacher. Mistake is the portal to discovery."

*****

"A quote has the power to change fate, change a person, and to change your mind."

*****

"A quote is a book but shortened and made so the average person can understand it."

*****

"A dream deferred in the soul, will never reveal genius that could have been showed. - Alex Murray

*****

"Courage is not the absence of fear but the judgement that something else is more important than fear."

*****

"I'm not a vegetarian because I like animals but because I hate plants."

*****

"Great oaks from little acorns grow."

*****

"Add one small bit to the truth and you inevitably subtract from it."

*****

"Life isn't about finding yourself. Life is about creating yourself." - George Bernard Shaw

*****

"Whenever I feel the need to exercise, I lie down until it goes away." - Paul Terry

*****

"As I walk through the valley of the shadow of death, I shall fear no evil, for I am the baddest mother f***er in the whole damn valley."

*****

"Only in their dreams can men truly be free. It was always thus and always this will be."

*****

"Pain is sweet, I enjoy it because it lets me know that I am alive."

*****

"The only way a reporter should look at a politician is down. - Frank Kent

*****

"One should always be in love. That is the reason one should never marry." - Oscar Wilde

*****

"To be yourself you have to be somebody."
- Stanislaw Jerzy Lec

*****

"Propaganda is that branch of the art of lying which consists in nearly deceiving your friends without quite deceiving your enemies." - Frances Cornford

*****

"There is no moderation in religion, reason is always desecrated by religion." - Patrick Emin

*****

"Idealism is the noble toga that political gentlemen drape over their will to power." - Aldous Huxley

*****

"Capitalism is the worst enemy of humanity."
- Evo Morales

*****

"I've had a perfectly wonderful evening, but this wasn't it." - Groucho Marx

*****

"A compromise is the art of dividing a cake in such a way that everyone believes he has the biggest piece."
- Ludwig Erhard

*****

"Some smiles are not happy smiles, rather are they a way of crying with kindness." - Gabriela Mistral

*****

"I am always of the opinion with the learned, if they speak first." - William Congreve

*****

"Do not use that foreign word 'ideals'. We have that excellent Norwegian word 'lies'." - Henrik Ibsen

*****

"When people are free to do as they please, they usually imitate each other." - Eric Hoffer

*****

"Specialists are people who always repeat the same mistakes." - Walter Gopius

*****

"Here lies my wife: here let her lie! Now she's at rest, and so am I." - John Dryden

*****

"I love nature, I just don't want to get any of it on me." - Woody Allen

*****

"When you were born you were crying whilst everyone around you was smiling, live your life so that when you die, you are smiling and everyone around you is crying."

*****

"Heresy is only another word for freedom of thought."
- Graham Greene

*****

"Anyone who maintains the ability to recognize beauty will never grow old." - Franz Kafka

*****

"Facts are always popping up to confuse the theories."
- Carlo Dossi

*****

"The only function of economic forecasting is to make astrology look respectable." - John Kenneth Galbraith

*****

"The political left is an evil that only the presence of the right makes tolerable." - Massimo D'Alema

*****

"So beautiful was she that they had forbidden her to approach the Leaning Tower of Pisa."

*****

"You know you're getting old when you stoop to tie your shoelaces and wonder what else you could do while your down there." - George Burns

*****

"Christ died for our sins. Dare we make his martyrdom meaningless by not committing them?"
- Jules Feiffer

*****

"If you can't explain it simply, you don't understand it well enough." - Albert Einstein

*****

"If your student isn't learning, you're not teaching."
- Mark Ziaian

*****

"What we call 'progress' is the exchange of one nuisance for another nuisance." - Havelock Ellis

*****

"A jury consists of twelve persons chosen to decide who has the better lawyer." - Robert Frost

*****

"The human race has one really effective weapon, and that is laughter." - Mark Twain

*****

"Governments never learn. Only people learn."
- Milton Friedman

*****

"Those are my principles, and if you don't like them...well I have others." - Groucho Marx

*****

"War is delightful to those who have had no experience of it." - Desiderius Erasmus

*****

"Idealism increases in direct proportion to one's distance from the problem." - John Galsworthy

*****

"No woman can endure a gambling husband, unless he is a steady winner." - Thomas Dewar

*****

"Be not afraid of greatness. Some are born great, some achieve greatness, and others have greatness thrust upon them." - William Shakespeare

*****

"Necessity has no law." - Oliver Cromwell

*****

"I think, therefore I am." - René Descartes

*****

"We don't see things as they are, we see them as we are." - Anaïs Nin

*****

"The future belongs to people who see possibilities before they become obvious." - Ted Levitt

*****

"The most dangerous food is wedding cake."
- James Thurber

*****

"When I was younger I could remember anything, whether it happened or not." - Mark Twain

*****

"War has no winners, just lesser losers."
- Mark Ziaian

*****

"War is God's way of teaching Americans geography." - Ambrose Bierce

*****

"Life can be wonderful if it doesn't frighten you."
- Charlie Chaplin

*****

"Learn from the mistakes of others. You can never live long enough to make them all yourself."
- Groucho Marx

*****

"It's when we forget ourselves that we do things which deserve to be remembered."

*****

"Let us enrich ourselves with our mutual differences."
- Paul Valéry

*****

"I am not young enough to know everything."
- Oscar Wilde

*****

"Almost all physicians have their favourite diseases."
- Henry Fielding

*****

"A fiancé is a happy man who is ready to cease being so." - Enrique Jardiel Poncela

*****

"Increase in wisdom can be measured accurately by the corresponding decrease in anger."
- Friedrich Nietzsche

*****

"People are only ridiculous when they want to appear or to be what they are not." - Giacomo Leopardi

*****

"I'm not afraid of death; I just don't want to be there when it happens." - Woody Allen

*****

"He hoisted his own flag high, so that he didn't have to look at it." - Stanislaw Jerzy Lec

*****

"There is only one thing in the world worse than being talked about, and that is not being talked about."
- Oscar Wilde

*****

"The poor go to war to fight and die for the whims, wealth and excesses of others." - Plutarch

*****

"It's better not to have laws than to break them every day." - Ugo Foscolo

*****

"A lawyer is a gentleman who rescues your estate from your enemies and keeps it for himself."
- Lord Henry Brougham

*****

"A dictionary is the whole universe arranged in alphabetical order." - Anatole France

*****

"The only beautiful eyes are those that look at you with tenderness." - Coco Chanel

*****

"There is only one success - to be able to spend your life in your own way." - Christopher Morley

*****

"Development is like a dead star whose light we can still see, even though it has been dead for ages and for ever." - Gilbert Rist

*****

"The dread of loneliness is greater than the fear of bondage, so we get married." - Cyril Connolly

*****

"The single biggest problem in communication is the illusion that it has taken place."
- George Bernard Shaw

*****

"Silence is gold, if nothing better you hold."
- Mark Ziaian

*****

"Start every day with a smile and get it over with."
- W.C. Fields

*****

"I find television very educating. Every time somebody turns on the set, I go into the other room and read a book." - Groucho Marx

*****

"Holding on to anger is like grasping a hot coal with the intent of throwing it at someone else; you are the one who gets burned." - Buddha

*****

"I'm such a good lover because I practice a lot on my own." - Woody Allen

*****

"I honestly think it is better to be a failure at something you love than to be a success at something you hate." - George Burns

*****

"We are learning by bitter experience that the organism which destroys its environment destroys itself." - Gregory Bateson

*****

"This we know: the earth does not belong to man, man belongs to the earth. All things are connected like the blood that unites us all. Man did not weave the web of life, he is merely a strand in it. Whatever he does to the web, he does to himself." - Chief Seattle

*****

"An optimist is he who believes that things cannot get any worse." - Alessandro Morandotti

*****

"A man, any man, is worth more than a flag, any flag." - Eduardo Chillida

*****

"A cynic is a man who, when he smells flowers, looks around for a coffin." - H.L. Mencken

*****

"The duration of passion is proportionate with the original resistance of the woman." - Honoré de Balzac

*****

"Keep your eyes wide open before marriage, half shut afterwards." - Benjamin Franklin

*****

"People never lie so much as before an election, during a war, or after a hunt." - Otto von Bismarck

*****

"Who are you to judge the life I live? I know I'm not perfect and I don't live to be, but before you start pointing fingers... make sure you hands are clean!"
- Bob Marley

*****

"I believe there is something out there watching us. Unfortunately, it's the government." - Woody Allen

*****

"The best way to learn how to make a film is to make one." - Stanley Kubrick

*****

"To improve one's style means to improve one's way of thinking." - Friedrich Nietzsche

*****

"One never goes so far as when one doesn't know where one is going." - Johann Wolfgang von Goethe

*****

"I have nothing but respect for you - and not much of that." - Groucho Marx

*****

"Nothing matters very much, and few things matter at all." - Arthur James Balfour

*****

"If I had a flower for every time I thought of you... I could walk through my garden forever."
- Alfred Tennyson

*****

"The divine light blinds the world instead of illuminating it." - Patrick Emin

*****

"Our lives end the day we become silent about things that really matter." - Martin Luther King

*****

"Hell, I never vote for anybody, I always vote against." - W.C. Fields

*****

"I intend to live forever, or die trying."
- Groucho Marx

*****

"Education is the most powerful weapon which you can use to change the world." - Nelson Mandela

*****

"The more you know, the more you know you don't know." - Aristotle

*****

"Keep away from people who try to belittle your ambitions. Small people always do that, but the really great make you feel that you, too, can become great."
- Mark Twain

*****

"Folks are usually about as happy as they make their minds up to be." - Abraham Lincoln

*****

"Sex at 90 is like shooting pool with a rope."
- George Burns

*****

"I can resist everything but temptation." - Oscar Wilde

*****

"I have great faith in fools. Self-confidence, my friends call it." – Edgar Allan Poe

*****

"Never tell the truth to people who are not worthy of it." - Mark Twain

*****

"It's the possibility of having a dream come true that makes life interesting." - Paulo Coelho

*****

"I love mankind ... it's people I can't stand!"
- Charles M. Schulz

*****

"Not all of us can do great things. But we can do small things with great love." - Mother Teresa

*****

"I don't know the question, but sex is definitely the answer." - Woody Allen

*****

"Some people think football is a matter of life and death. I can assure you it's much more serious than that." - Bill Shankly

*****

"An eye for an eye will only make the whole world blind." - Mahatma Gandhi

*****

"Be careful about reading health books. Some fine day you'll die of a misprint." - Markus Herz

*****

"If you're gonna be two-faced at least make one of them pretty." - Marilyn Monroe

*****

"A day without laughter is a day wasted."
- Charlie Chaplin

*****

"I speak to everyone in the same way, whether he is the garbage man or the president of the university."
- Albert Einstein

*****

"Intelligent people find it difficult to communicate with ordinary people. Very intelligent people don't."
- Mark Ziaian

*****

"One good thing about music, when it hits you, you feel no pain." - Bob Marley

*****

"Perhaps one did not want to be loved so much as to be understood." - George Orwell

****

"A lie can travel half way around the world while the truth is putting on its shoes." - Mark Twain

*****

"Those who don't believe in magic will never find it."
- Roald Dahl

*****

"May you live all the days of your life."
- Jonathan Swift

*****

"A clever person solves a problem. A wise person avoids it." - Albert Einstein

*****

"She got her looks from her father. He's a plastic surgeon." - Groucho Marx

*****

"Going to church doesn't make you a Christian any more than going to a garage makes you an automobile." - Billy Sunday

*****

"The purpose of our lives is to be happy."
- The Dalai Lama, Tenzin Gyatso

*****

"Many of life's failures are people who did not realize how close they were to success when they gave up."
- Thomas A. Edison

*****

"And, when you want something, all the universe conspires in helping you to achieve it." - Paulo Coelho

*****

"I am free of all prejudice. I hate everyone equally."
- W.C. Fields

*****

"And those who were seen dancing were thought to be insane by those who could not hear the music."
- Friedrich Nietzsche

*****

"Whoever is happy will make others happy too."
- Anne Frank

*****

"There is nothing to writing. All you do is sit down at a typewriter and bleed." - Ernest Hemingway

*****

"A change of work is just like a rest."
- Thomas W. Dorsey

*****

"Nothing is impossible to a willing heart."
- John Heywood

*****

"Women are made to be loved, not understood."
- Oscar Wilde

*****

"Two things are infinite, the universe and human stupidity." - Albert Einstein

*****

"You don't love someone because they're perfect, you love them in spite of the fact that they're not."
- Jodi Picoult

*****

"Creativity is allowing oneself to make mistakes. Art is knowing which ones to keep." - Scott Adams

*****

"Behind every successful man there's a lot of unsuccessful years." - Bob Brown

*****

"Those who believe in telekinetics, raise my hand!"
- Kurt Vonnegut

*****

"Progress is impossible without change."
- George Bernard Shaw

*****

"Facts do not cease to exist because they are ignored."
- Aldous Huxley

*****

"May you live every day of your life."
- Jonathan Swift

*****

"Love is friendship set to music." - Joseph Campbell

*****

"A smile is a curve that sets everything straight."
- Phyllis Diller

*****

"It was a woman who drove me to drink, and I never had the courtesy to thank her for it." - W.C. Fields

*****

"You talk when you cease to be at peace with your thoughts." - Kahlil Gibran

*****

"Where there is love there is life." - Mahatma Gandhi

*****

"The difference between genius and stupidity is: genius has its limits." - Alexandre Dumas-fils

*****

"Some infinities are bigger than other infinities."
- John Green,

*****

"Always be sincere, even if you don't mean it."
- Harry S. Truman

*****

"Quote me as saying I was mis-quoted."
- Groucho Marx

*****

"If you don't know where you're going, any road'll take you there" - George Harrison

*****

"When darkness comes, and pain is all around,
like a bridge over troubled water, I will lay me down."
- Paul Simon

*****

"In 1969 I gave up women and alcohol. It was the
worst 20 minutes of my life." - George Best

*****

"Be yourself; everyone else is already taken."
- Oscar Wilde

*****

"American by birth, Southern by the grace of God."

*****

"Your quote is only a quote when someone else
mentions it. You can quote me on that." - Mark Ziaian

*****

INDEX

Adams, Douglas, 6
Adams, Franklin Pierce,
  36
Adams, Scott, 100
Ali, Muhammad, 74
Allen, Woody, 3, 53, 83,
  89, 91, 93, 96
American Pie, 9
Angelou, Maya, 78
Aristotle, 94
Aurelius, Marcus, 38, 39
Balfour, Arthur James,
  93
Bateson, Gregory, 91
Best, George, 102
Biagi, Enzo, 53
Bibb, Leslie, 19
Bierce, Ambrose, 87
Bowen, James, 75
Braveheart, 62
Braxton, Tony, 2
Brougham, Lord Henry,
  89
Brown, Bob, 100
Brown, Les, 25
Buddha, 91
Buechner, Carl W, 39
Burns, George, 84, 91, 95
Buscaglia, Leo, 2

Butler, Samuel, 20
Campbell, Joseph, 100
Camus, Albert, 1
Carr, Caleb, 7
Chanel, Coco, 30, 90
Chaplin, Charlie, 87, 96
Chillida, Eduardo, 92
City High, 11
Cloud, Henry, 29
Cocteau, Jean, 67
Coelho, Paulo, 95, 98
Confucius, 2
Congreve, William, 83
Connolly, Cyril, 90
Cornford, Frances, 82
Cromwell, Oliver, 86
Crow T. Robot, 41
Da Vinci, Leonardo, 66
Dahl, Roald, 97
D'Alema, Massimo, 84
de Balzac, Honoré, 92
Descartes, René, 86
Dewar, Thomas, 86
Dickson, Jake, 61
Dietrich, Marlene, 24
Diller, Phyllis, 100
Dinges, Robert, 6
DMX, 14
Dodson, Fitzhugh, 26

Dorsey, Thomas W, 99
Dossi, Carlo, 84
Dr Seuss, 3, 77
Dryden, John, 83
Du Bois, W.E.B, 59
Dumas-fils, Alexandre, 101
Eban, Abba, 45
Edison, Thomas A, 98
Einstein, Albert, 1, 23, 37, 39, 66, 73, 85, 96, 97, 99
Ellis, Havelock, 85
Emerson, Ralph Waldo, 1
Emin, Patrick, 82, 94
Erasmus, Desiderius, 86
Erhard, Ludwig, 82
Feiffer, Jules, 85
Fielding, Henry, 88
Fields, W.C, 90, 94, 98, 101
Foscolo, Ugo, 89
Frame, Janet, 54
France, Anatole, 89
Frank, Anne, 99
Franklin, Benjamin, 60, 92
Friedman, Milton, 85
Frost, David, 29
Frost, Robert, 65, 85
Galbraith, John Kenneth, 84
Galilei, Galileo, 43
Gallagher, Noel, 2

Galsworthy, John, 86
Gandhi, Mahatma, 96, 101
General Chang, 7
Gibran, Kahlil, 101
Goldsmith, Oliver, 37
Gopius, Walter, 83
Green, John, 6, 101
Greene, Graham, 84
Hackers, 65
Harrison, George, 101
Hebert, John, 58
Heinlein, Robert A, 19, 75
Hemingway, Ernest, 31, 99
Herodotus, 14
Herz, Markus, 96
Heywood, John, 99
Hitler, Adolf, 31
Hoffer, Eric, 83
Hope, Anthony, 66
Hugli, Yvonne, 38
Huxley, Aldous, 82, 100
Ibsen, Henrik, 83
Insull, Samuel, 26
Joel, Billy, 73
Johnson, Samuel, 51
Joplin, Janis, 3
Kafka, Franz, 84
Katt, Tommy D, 10
Kent, Frank, 81
King, Martin Luther, 10, 94

Kozol, Johnathan, 66
Krystal Sundstrom-
  Hebert, 59
Kubrick, Stanley, 93
Lec, Stanislaw Jerzy, 1,
  81, 89
Lee, Robert E, 38
Leopardi, Giacomo, 88
Levitt, Ted, 87
Lincoln, Abraham, 11,
  63, 95
Lombardi, Vince, 5
M*A*S*H, 60
Maclean, Norman, 63
Madonna, 16
Mandela, Nelson, 94
Marley, Bob, 92, 97
Marx, Groucho, 40, 82,
  86, 87, 91, 93, 94, 98,
  101
Maxim, Cadet, 37
McDowell, Josh, 68
Mencken, H.L., 92
Michelangelo, 63
Milani, Lorenzo, 31
Mistral, Gabriela, 82
Monroe, Marilyn, 96
Morales, Evo, 82
Morandotti, Alessandro,
  57, 92
Morley, Christopher, 90
Mother Teresa, 19, 72, 95
Moulin Rouge, 59
Mullins, Rich, 67

Murphy, Gwen, 43
Murray, Alex, 80
Napoleon, 37
Nietzsche, Friedrich, 1,
  38, 88, 93, 98
Nin, Anaïs, 5, 86
Oklahoma the musical,
  29
Orwell, George, 97
Paredes, Ana, 41
Perkins, Alex, 42
Picasso, Pablo, 78
Picoult, Jodi, 99
Plutarch, 89
Poe, Edgar Allan, 95
Poncela, Enrique Jardiel,
  88
Proverbs
  African, 58
  Akan, 58
  Ancient, 52
  Arab, 20
  Japanese, 67
  Klingon, 6
  Portuguese, 67
  Texan, 68
  Yiddish, 66
Rabelais, François, 12
Rist, Gilbert, 90
Rocky Horror Picture
  Show, 41
Roosevelt, Eleanor, 43
Roosevelt, Franklin D,
  24, 37

Roosevelt, Theodore, 36, 68
Rossi, Father Bernie, 40
Ruth, Babe, 20
Sandler, Adam, 48
Schulz, Charles M, 77, 95
Scream, 49
Seattle, Chief, 91
Seida, Kathy, 4
Selva, Angelo, 40
Shakespeare, William, 5, 6, 33, 42, 86
Shakur, Tupac, 12, 13, 44, 71
Shankly, Bill, 96
Shaw, Carrie, 5
Shaw, George Bernard, 57, 80, 90, 100
Simon, Paul, 102
Snipes, Wesley, 22
Socrates, 52
Spock, 14
Squally, White, 62
St. James, Rebecca, 33
Stefani, Gwen, 19
Stein, Gertrude, 56
Sunday, Billy, 98
Swift, Jonathan, 60, 97, 100
Tennyson, Alfred, 93
Terry, Paul, 81
The Beatles, 15, 59

The Bible, 5, 35, 51, 66, 67
The Dalai Lama, 98
The Rock, 5
The Usual Suspects, 65
Thoreau, Henry, 67
Thumper, 69
Thurber, James, 87
Tracy, Brian, 25
Truman, Harry S, 101
Twain, Mark, 2, 39, 85, 87, 94, 95, 97
Twisted Metal, 33
Tzu, Sun, 35
Updike, John, 17
Valéry, Paul, 88
Van Dyken, Amy, 78
Voltaire, 8, 38
von Bismarck, Otto, 92
von Goethe, Johann Wolfgang, 93
Vonnegut, Kurt, 100
Washington, George, 57
Waters, Roger, 73
Wilde, Oscar, 13, 30, 68, 81, 88, 89, 95, 99, 102
Wizard of Oz, 20
Wrigley, William, 9
Yoda, 44, 47
Zappa, Frank, 23
Ziaian, Mark, 44, 58, 85, 87, 90, 97, 102
Ziaian, Shodja, 70

www.ingramcontent.com/pod-product-compliance
Lightning Source LLC
Chambersburg PA
CBHW032116280326
41933CB00009B/858